Questions Kids Ask About God

By David Hedlin

Illustrated by

Lillian Krieger

Jacob Brown

Courtney Paarlberg

Matthew 19:14 "Jesus said, 'Let the children come to me and do not stop them, because the kingdom of heaven belongs to such as these.' "

Questions Kids Ask About God

Copyright 2012, 2013, 2015 © QKA Publishing, New Lenox, Illinois

ISBN 978-0-9835627-0-2
Library of Congress Control Number 2011904996

Published September 2012, First Edition
Printed and bound in the United States of America.

Hi! I'm Pastor Dave,

When I was growing up, the church was always an important part of my family life. As a kid, I thought about being a pastor. A pastor helps people learn more about God.

To become a pastor, I had to go to school for many years. After college, I went to a special school called "seminary." There I learned more about serving God.

I felt this was my "calling" from God. It is what he wants me to do with my life. God has a "calling" for each of us. Some of us grow up to be teachers, carpenters, salespeople, musicians or stay-at-home moms and dads. Whatever you are called to do with your life, God can use you to make a difference in the world.

As pastor of Peace Lutheran Church, kids come to me with lots of great questions. Kids are not afraid to ask some of the questions that even adults wonder about. During church services, we have a special time when I answer "Questions Kids Ask." This book shares some of those questions.

This is only the beginning. I hope this book gives families an opportunity to talk about God, explore the Bible, become closer to Jesus, and ask more questions.

Pastor Dave Hedlin
Peace Lutheran Church, New Lenox, Illinois

Can you find the doves ⚘ in this book? There are 7 doves.
God's love and peace are everywhere!

Who is God?

God is love. He made
all things because he loves us.
We are all children of God.

1 John 4:7 & 8 "Dear friends, let us love one another, because love comes from God. Whoever loves is a child of God and knows God. Whoever does not love does not know God, for God is love."

How old is God?

God doesn't keep track of time like we do. He has no age, no height, and no weight. God just is. God has always been there and he will always be there.

Where is God ?

You can't find God on a map. God doesn't have an address, a phone number or a website.

There is no place we can go to see or touch God, but we can feel God's love with us everywhere.

Does God watch us all the time?

YES! God watches over us
when we play with our friends and go to school. He sees us
eat our snacks and pick up our toys. God is there when we
go to sleep and when we wake up. He always watches over us.

Scientists have studied the earth and know that dinosaurs lived before people. God created people a long, long time after the dinosaurs were gone.

Why did God make mosquitoes suck my blood?

Mosquitoes suck our blood-it's what they eat. They may bug us and make us itch! God's world includes all kinds of critters. Each one has a reason for living. Perhaps God made mosquitoes so frogs, birds and fish have something to eat for lunch.

1 Timothy 4:4a "Everything that God created is good; nothing is to be rejected..."

What is God's favorite animal?

God doesn't have a favorite animal. He made the animals and loves them all. Each one is special - some chirp, some gallop, some slither.

Genesis 1:24a & 25 "Then God commanded, 'Let the earth produce all kinds of animal life...' So God made them all, and he was pleased with what he saw."

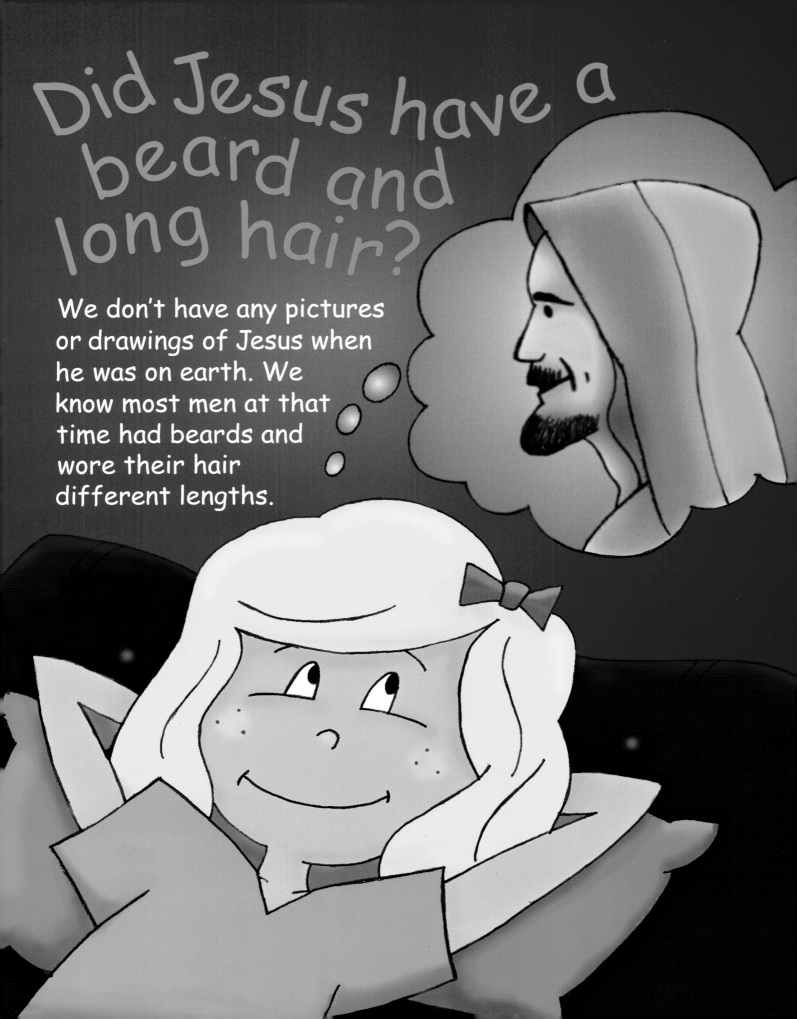

Did Jesus have a beard and long hair?

We don't have any pictures or drawings of Jesus when he was on earth. We know most men at that time had beards and wore their hair different lengths.

What is the Bible?

The Bible is a big book made up of 66 smaller books. It was written by lots of people over many years. The Bible is bursting with all kinds of cool stories about animals, adventures, and families.

What does God's handwriting look like?

God doesn't use pencils, paper or a computer. Instead, God inspires people.

He gives us the ability to tell others about him. We do that by writing, drawing, singing, and sometimes just by talking! People are sort of like God's handwriting.

Revelation 21:3b-4a "Now God's home is with people! He will live with them, and they shall be his people. He will wipe away all tears from their eyes."

Heaven is wherever God is. The Bible says that it is more beautiful than any place on earth. It is full of God's love. In heaven, everyone is happy and no one is sick or sad.

What is prayer?

Prayer is talking to God. We can tell God anything. We don't need to say the words out loud. Sometimes we can just be quiet and think about God.

1 Thessalonians 5:16-18a "Be joyful always, pray at all times, be thankful in all circumstances."

How can God listen to all those prayers at once?

Thank you for watching over me...

Dear God, I thank you for...

I know you are always listening...

God bless my family and friends for loving me...

We don't understand how God does it, but he does. He can do anything. God put billions of stars in the sky. Each grain of sand and each snow-flake he makes is different. He can also listen to all our prayers at once.

God is awesome!

Psalms 66:19 "But God has indeed heard me; he has listened to my prayer."

What's the best way to pray?

It doesn't matter how we pray. We can pray with our family, friends or alone. We can pray during the day or in the middle of the night. We can pray at home, school, church or a ball game. We can even pray on a roller coaster. Just pray!

Colossians 4:2 "Be persistent in prayer and keep alert as you pray, giving thanks to God."

What should we pray for?

God likes us to talk to him about everything in our life- happy or sad.

We can pray to say thank you or ask for his help. Prayer brings us closer to God. It helps us learn what God wants us to do.

Philippians 4:6 "Don't worry about anything, but in all your prayers ask God for what you need, always asking him with a thankful heart."

What does God want me to do?

God wants all of us to love him. He also wants us to love and take care of other people and his world.

We can be like a light, shining God's love to those around us. Say to yourself, "I'm going to be God's helper today." See what good things you can do.

Matthew 5:16 "In the same way your light must shine before people so that they will see the good things you do and praise your father in heaven."

". . . give peace to your Church, peace among nations, peace in our homes, and peace in our hearts; through your Son, Jesus Christ our Lord. Amen."

If you would like to order additional copies of *Questions Kids Ask About God* contact us:

QKA Publishing
P.O. Box 205
New Lenox, Illinois 60451

Website: www.qkapublishing.com

Peace Lutheran Church is grateful for all kids asking questions!

A special thanks to Paul Faris for his art and design direction.

Thank you to our following illustrators:

Jacob Brown
Lillian Krieger
Courtney Paarlberg

We would also like to acknowledge:

Pastor Dave Hedlin
Jennifer Arthur
Susan DeMar Lafferty
Carol Hedlin
Eric Leslie Sperstad
Lynn Taeger-Peterson

All proceeds from this book will be used to support children's ministries around the world.